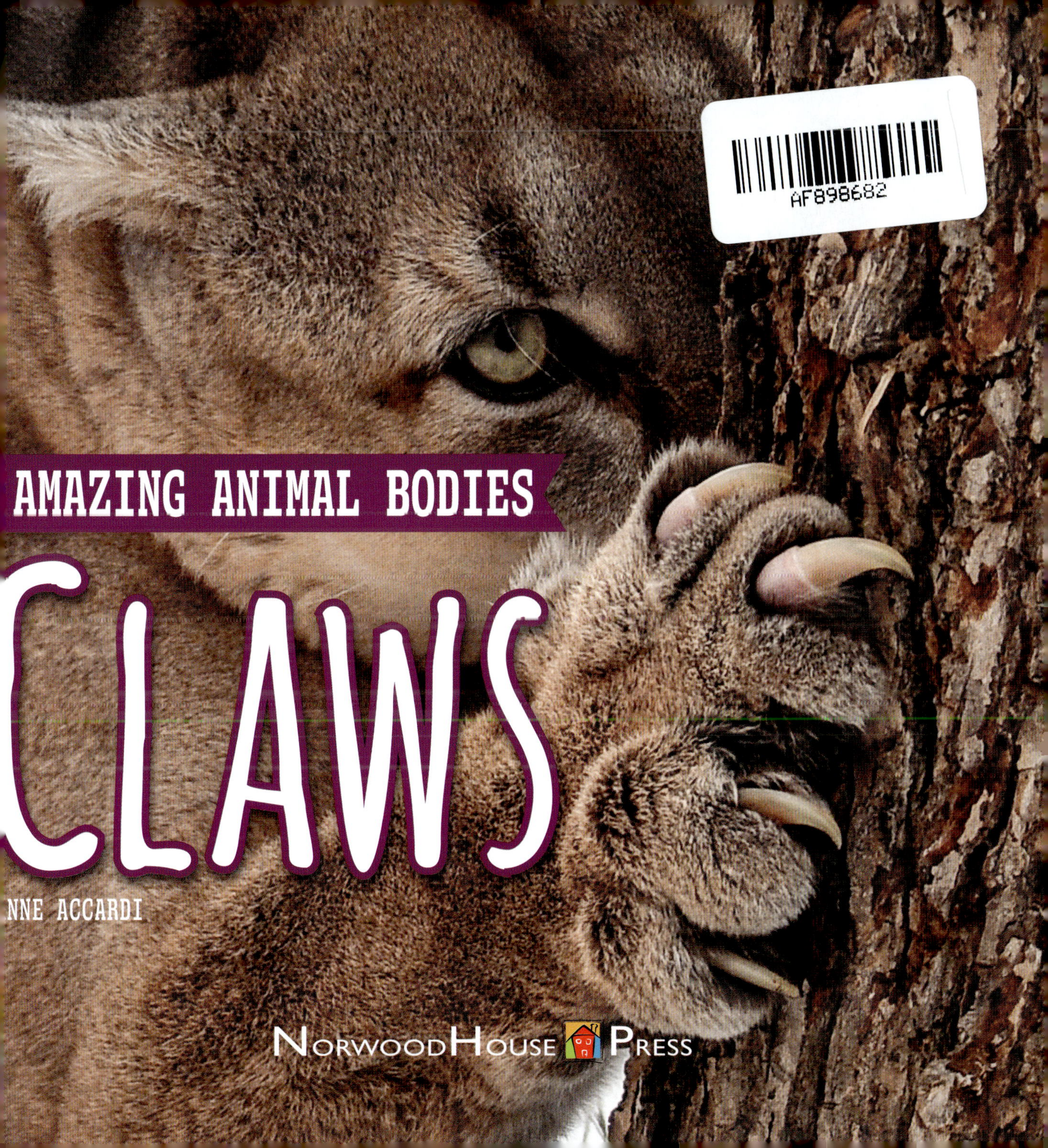

AMAZING ANIMAL BODIES

CLAWS

NNE ACCARDI

NorwoodHouse Press

Cataloging-in-Publication Data

Names: Accardi, Anne.
Title: Claws / Anne Accardi.
Description: Buffalo, NY : Norwood House Press, 2027. | Series: Amazing animal bodies | Includes glossary and index.
Identifiers: ISBN 9781978579514 (pbk.) | ISBN 9781978579521 (library bound) | ISBN 9781978579538 (ebook)
Subjects: LCSH: Claws--Juvenile literature.
Classification: LCC QL942.A33 2027 | DDC 591.47--dc23

Published in 2027 by
Norwood House Press
2544 Clinton Street
Buffalo, NY 14224

Designer: Rhea Magaro
Editor: Kim Thompson

Photo credits: Cover, p. 1 Michael Cola/Shutterstock.com; p. 5 Michal Varga/Shutterstock.com; p. 6 Okyela/Shutterstock.com; p. 9 Zajac Software Ltd/Shutterstock.com; pp. 10, 11 Patrick Messier/Shutterstock.com; p. 12 Various images/Shutterstock.com; p. 13 Lumin Heart Studio/Shutterstock.com; p. 14 jivagoz/Shutterstock.com; p. 15 Wondry/Shutterstock.com; p. 17 Jukka Jantunen/Shutterstock.com; p. 18 jindrich_pavelka/Shutterstock.com; p. 20 OSDG/Shutterstock.com; p. 21 RLS Photo/Shutterstock.com;

Printed in the United States of America

CPSIA compliance information: Batch #CSNHP27: For further information contact Norwood House Press at 1-800-237-9932.

TABLE OF CONTENTS

What Are Claws?

Claws are body parts. Many animals have them. They grow on an animal's feet or **paws**.

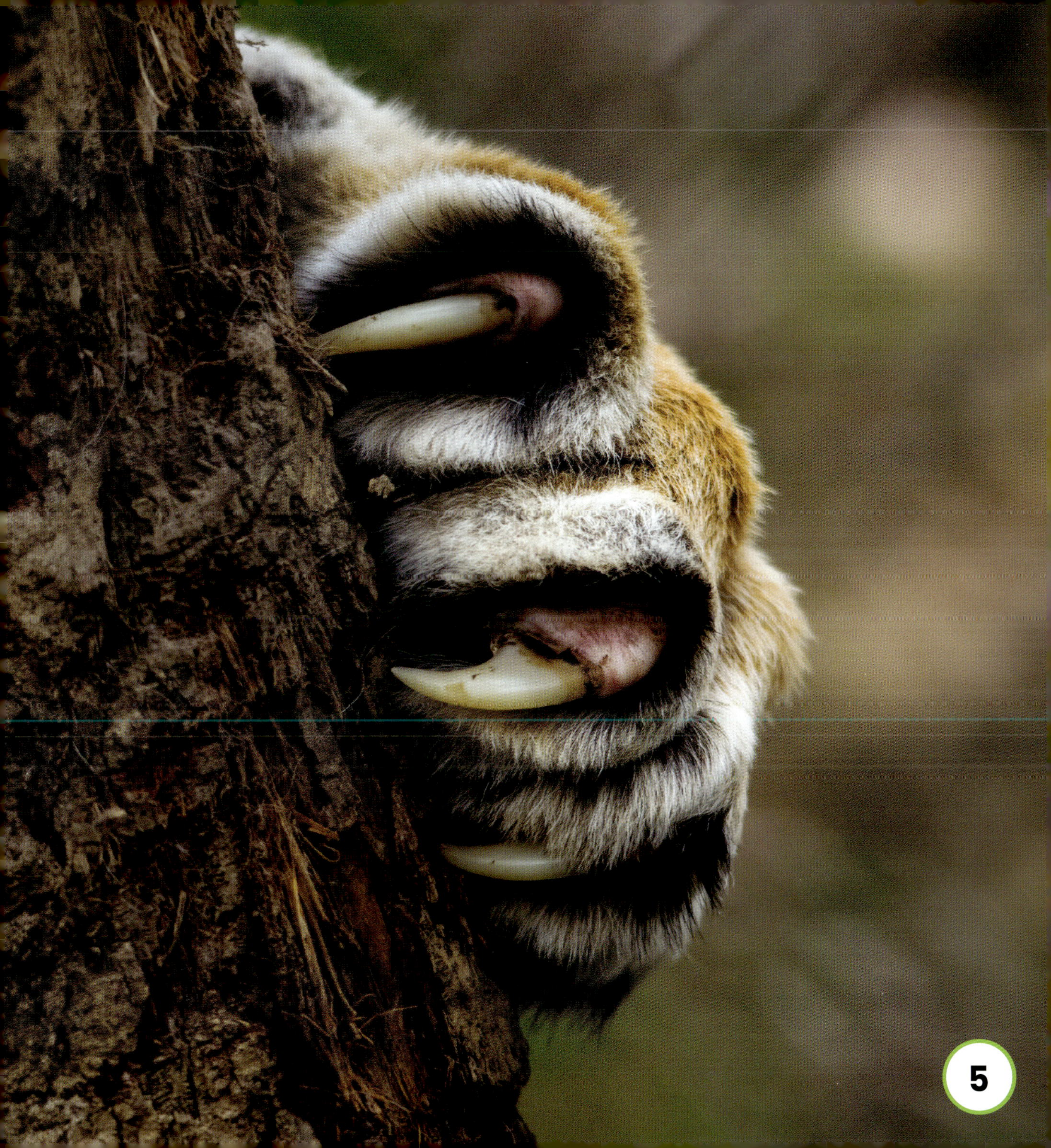

Most claws are sharp. Some are curved like hooks. Some claws **retract**. Others stay in place.

Cat Claws

When a cat scratches something, its claws leave a smell. The mark tells other animals to stay away!

Eagle Claws

An eagle's claws are called **talons**. An eagle swoops down with its talons out.

The talons grab **prey**.

They crush and kill.

Bear Claws

Black bears dig with their claws.

They find tasty bugs in the dirt.

They build **dens**.

A polar bear's claws grip the ice.

Sloth Claws

A sloth has long, curved claws.

They hold on to trees.

They help sloths hang upside down!

Beaver Claws

Beavers use claws for **grooming**. Their claws smooth fur. They pull out bugs.

Honey Badger Claws

Honey badgers love to get honey.

Their claws open **beehives**.

Their claws also attack enemies.

They slash at lions and leopards.

Lobster Claws

A lobster has two claws. One is **blunt** and heavy. It crushes prey.

The other claw is sharp. It rips and tears food.

Glossary

beehives (BEE-hives): nests where swarms of bees live and make honey

blunt (bluhnt): dull; not sharp

dens (dens): the homes of wild animals, often dug into the ground

grooming (GROO-ming): combing, brushing, and cleaning

paws (pawz): the feet of animals that have four feet

prey (pray): animals eaten by other animals

retract (ri-TRAKT): to pull back or in; to draw back

talons (TAL-uhnz): sharp, curved claws on a bird of prey such as an eagle or hawk

Thinking Questions

1. Where are claws found on an animal's body?
2. What are talons?
3. How do a bear's claws help it live?
4. Does a honey badger have sharp claws? How do you know?
5. Describe a lobster's claws.

Index

About the Author

Anne Accardi is a librarian who loves reading books and learning new things! She lives in Kansas City, Missouri. When she's not writing, Anne enjoys listening to music, exploring nature around the city, and spending time with her family.